ABANDONED NORTH ALABAMA

MARY POSEY

AMERICA THROUGH TIME®
ADDING COLOR TO AMERICAN HISTORY

America Through Time is an imprint of Fonthill Media LLC
www.through-time.com
office@through-time.com

Published by Arcadia Publishing by arrangement with Fonthill Media LLC
For all general information, please contact Arcadia Publishing:
Telephone: 843-853-2070
Fax: 843-853-0044
E-mail: sales@arcadiapublishing.com
For customer service and orders:
Toll-Free 1-888-313-2665

www.arcadiapublishing.com

First published 2020

ISBN 978-1-63499-245-9

Typeset in Trade Gothic
Printed and bound in England

CONTENTS

ACKNOWLEDGMENTS

I'd like to give an enormous thank you to Robert Posey, Lacey Posey, and Karen Allison—my scouting partners and biggest supporters of this endeavor, who came along with me to sketchy neighborhoods and isolated places. We lived to see another day! And to my parents Jim and Annette Albert, who encouraged me and supported me and have been my biggest fans my entire life no matter the endeavor. My dad passed before I started this journey, but he once kept a speeding ticket simply because it had my name on it, I know he would be tremendously excited about the manifestation of something real coming to fruition. Mom, I want anyone who happens to pick this up to know how proud I am of you and your strength to continue so beautifully on your own. You are living every day true to yourself and I couldn't be happier for you. "Are you living or are you simply existing?" We will choose to live, come rain or shine.

INTRODUCTION: THERE'S ALWAYS A PIANO

Blink. Read this or don't. Time is passing either way. This blinking cursor of mine is counting the seconds for you, and for me. If you think of time in such small increments, you'll find yourself paralyzed. Unable to move forward and hypnotized by the illusion of it standing still. If instead you think of time in increments that are impossibly large, you'll find yourself with the same cinder blocks stuck to your feet like a recurring dream you can't wake yourself from despite your best efforts. But for what it's worth, I've found that if you trudge ahead, your forward momentum will help keep you moving. And movement is your saving grace. Stall to watch the cursor blink and you're stuck again. Lucky for the writer types, there's the luxury of a backspace button should you come to dislike what you've done thus far. If only life would allow for such a simple undo. Wishing and hoping for things to be seems to be our fatal flaw. I should follow my own advice. But this book isn't a self-help book. This book isn't a story. This book isn't a history lesson. This book is mostly about time and how anything left to its own devices will relinquish its sovereignty as time does what it will. Falling prey to stagnation is your first and biggest mistake. Typically, what time does to things isn't pretty. It will simply destroy whatever isn't actively fighting against it.

I've come across seven pianos along this journey. There's always a piano. Their weight and mass make relocating them more trouble than they're worth to those who are incapable of understanding how to make them sing. As soon as the music stops, they're left to rot. Stagnation will always be the biggest mistake.

1

THE VINTAGE STATION

Not knowing exactly where I was going, following directions called out by my phone, I found myself in the middle of an unexpectedly populated area. The roads were busy, but the parking lot was desolate as if there was really no need for its existence. The story of the Vintage Station is as beautiful as it is sinister. Depending on who you ask, it's either a story of faith and hope or a story of conspiracy and murder.

Standing inside the remains of the depot, your breath is taken by the trains that rip past. Located in the old Bessemer Freight Depot, the second oldest building in Bessemer, Alabama, the Vintage Station opened in 2014 and specialized in salvaged materials for custom furniture and remodeling. More specifically, it specialized in furniture and doors made from reclaimed wood and ironwork. Much the opposite of the forgotten places you'll read about in the coming chapters, Vintage Station took what was once discarded and turned it into beautiful, desirable pieces of art. Ravaged by fire, what's left behind speaks to everyone who visits. Beautiful stained-glass windows still largely intact glimmer in the sunlight. The pieces of glass that are missing provide an easy entrance for crawling vines, breaking the colorful consistency and filling it with green. The beauty that remains in the station, despite its unhappy ending, makes me wish I could build walls around it that would protect what has been persevered, despite its owner's absence. A wondrous place filled with remnants of masterful handiwork that just begs to be protected—like a memory of a lost loved one you can feel slipping through your fingers.

Owned by the late Brad Watkins, it also served as a ministry. Unemployed men were taught job skills and were provided counselling services. Winding up each workday with a prayer, Watkins was dedicated to his employees and his faith. In March of 2017, fire swept through the station, destroying the store building along with the inventory, machinery, and materials. The cause of the fire is still presently unknown. Watkins was quoted by al.com as saying, "We suffered a catastrophic loss last night. Tuesday March 27th, we had a fire that has destroyed a large portion of the building, all of our machinery and materials ... This, although heartbreaking, can be a beautiful story of renewal. A story of the body of Christ putting a marker in the ground and saying loudly, 'We will stand! We will not be defeated!'" Watkins moved the furniture building operation a few blocks away to fulfill outstanding orders and later reopened for a brief time in April. However, the business didn't survive through the year.

Ten months later, in 2018 at age fifty, Watkins would fall victim to a drive-by shooting. A stray bullet entered his room at a Fairfield hotel. Police said dozens of shots rang out and struck the hotel. Watkins was in a third-floor room when he was hit by a bullet that penetrated the wall. Shell casings scattered the roadway in front of the hotel. Employees worked to patch the glass door that lead to the lobby while investigations began.

Despite working to overcome his past, the nefarious circumstances surrounding Watkins might suggest to some that his death was no coincidence. Prior to owning the Vintage Station, in 2006 Watkins was arrested and charged for his role in an intricate drug scheme. Consumers were misled to believe they were purchasing legitimate prescription drugs from Canada at a cheaper rate. The pills were in fact from a home operation in South America. United States Attorney David Nahmias is quoted as saying, "The indictment's allegations are disturbing because customers thought they were getting legitimate and safe prescription drugs over the internet from Canada at cheaper prices, when in reality they received adulterated fakes that were crudely made in an unsanitary house in Belize." The drugs included unapproved versions of well-known and highly prescribed drugs such as Ambien, Valium, Xanax, Viagra, Cialis, Lipitor and Vioxx. According to Nahmias, from 2002 through 2004, the defendants allegedly ordered enough active ingredients to manufacture millions of pills.

Currently, the Vintage Station is still standing with most of its beautiful stained glass still intact. Satisfied customers still post pictures of exquisite pieces of furniture that found a home outside the walls of the depot. Regardless of where you fall on the details, the story of the Vintage Station is a tragic one. As of this writing, Watkins' murder remains unsolved.

The Vintage Station, formerly Bessemer Freight Depot.

View from the train tracks.

Above: Windows on the backside of the station.

Left: Beautiful stained-glass windows still largely intact inside the depot.

Vines creeping through the holes in the windows.

A view from the outside looking in.

Above left: Door left propped against the windows inside.

Above right: Looking out toward the tracks on a rainy day.

Above left: Chairs and files left behind.

Above right: Vines growing through the cracks framing gorgeously detailed vintage doorknobs.

Right: Closed indefinitely.

Below: More exquisite windows along the outside.

Amtrak trains rip past the defunct depot.

Hope persists, despite the sad circumstances surrounding the Vintage Station.

Pieces of things that were once for sale still remain inside the store area.

Locked inside the store, there are still things that were used for the furniture building operation.

2

1930S BUS

Right off the road, into the woods a little way at Guntersville State Park, there is a 1930s Trailways Chevy Beck bus with a tree growing through its hood. Determined to take its space, nature always wins. Tree beats metal. Long forgotten and unused, the bus has been left to rot. Adding insult to injury, the busted front window still has its windshield wipers. Lodged into the ground, the accordion-style door is perpetually open. According to the locals, no one knows exactly how it got there, but it has likely been there since the 1940s. It was left in what used to be a cow pasture. At one time, it was used as a personal residence; after that, it was gutted and made into a covered cattle trough. Occasionally these buses, no longer acceptable forms of transportation, were used for storage and discarded when no longer needed. Stripped of anything useful, the bus has been sitting among the trees for decades.

A tree growing through the hood of the bus. Nature always wins.

Gutted of anything of use.

Back window of the bus busted out.

Windshield wipers still holding on.

3

VALLEY HILL CHURCH OF GOD

A little rural church sits right off the road in tall grass that has not been maintained for quite some time. Once upon a time, cars surely lined up Sunday mornings in the ample space for parking. The familiar congregation would likely file in through the double doors to their regular seats, and feel amiss should a newcomer not realize where they happened to fall was already spoken for. Bless their hearts. Women of faith with study Bibles under their arms would dutifully wrangle restless children and beg for proper quiet and stillness. Men of faith (or a certain fear of the women of faith they married) might linger near the entrance until the preacher found his way to the front. Fidgety children would have second thoughts of misbehaving once they caught their mother's glare—despite their father's snoring through the service being the bigger distraction. Elbowing their father and glaring at the children throughout the sermon was certainly a full-time job. Time to stand. Time to sing. Time to sit and pray. Time to shake your neighbor's hand. Time to pray. Time for lunch. The children would dash to the adjacent yard and run after each other until their parents had finished dissecting the lives of everyone in town. Only then could they go to lunch.

As it sits now, devoid of churchgoers, the faded, musty pews have forgotten who belongs where. Restless children are surely by now anxious adults worrying over bills, weight gain, and knee replacements. Aside from its faithful congregation, the building still holds everything else you would expect to find in a rural church. The empty attendance board is testament to even the most ardent being evicted by the black mold that blankets the interior.

The rural church in an overgrown lot in Curry.

The piano at the front of the sanctuary, safe from the elements, is still upright with all of its ivory.

Pews still in place inside the church.

Empty attendance board.

Crucifix and Bible left behind.

Anointing oil still sitting on top of the piano.

At the pulpit.

At the altar.

Psalm 23 still framed and upright.

Chalkboard in the children's area.

Pastor's office.

Inside the pastor's office.

4

FORGOTTEN MACHINE SHOP

A railroad leads the way to an entrance near an old machine shop. Unable to continue this way because of the train, you must find an alternate route. Once there, inching your way just inside the broken doorway, a noise that sounds like other people moving around inside causes you to hesitate. "Others" can quickly be the downfall to any would-be explorer. Upon closer inspection, the noise is the wind blowing across VHS tape that's been streamed throughout the defunct building. Nonetheless, you feel like you're being watched. Each room you pass through leaves you uneasy and gives no relief to this invisible voyeur idea that your mind has conjured.

This abandoned machine shop in Huntsville leaves a lot to the imagination, but not much in the way of facts. Research on this shop proved futile in regard to what was actually manufactured here and even its name eluded me. Google can answer most questions for you if you dig long enough. Unfortunately, only two facts turned up during my search for information on this location: the manufacturing property contains 5,000 square feet and was built in 1975.

VHS tape strewn throughout the building.

Vandals turned an ordinary room into something from a horror movie.

View from upstairs looking down on the factory floor.

"Evil is here" tag is believable. The entire property leaves you feeling uneasy.

Above: Flower growing among the chaos.

Right: On the factory floor.

Side building on the property.

View from inside a side building looks like a large prison cell.

5

FORT McCLELLAN

Most of the time if you aren't out actively searching for forgotten pieces of the world around you, those pieces mostly go unnoticed. Drive down old country roads and notice the trees that line them. Sometimes you'll notice shadows fill in the space where typically light would filter through the leaves. Something behind them oddly blocks the sunlight and a darkness catches your eye. You can tell by gaps in the tops of them where land was once cleared for a structure and new trees have since overtaken it. New trees, vines, grass and briars slowly creep back to where they once had been, consuming the structure and shrouding it from plain sight. Nature reclaims what we discard.

Fort McClellan is an exception to this typical equation. It sits slightly off the main road with a nicely paved private drive that winds its way around the property that is still partly in use. The pristine landscape leads you to believe nothing is askew. Dozens of buildings sit along this drive; some are clearly still in use, but others are left mostly empty with their doors ajar. Neighborhood kids climbing on the stairs and fences of these unused buildings scatter when cars drive by. Inside the vacated buildings the air is thick and stagnant. Room after room, it fills your airways. Warm, humid conditions assure that everything stays covered in mold. The paint pulls away from the walls, reaching for a welcome breeze that never comes.

Fort McClellan was a United States Army post located in Anniston, Alabama. It operated from 1917 to 1995 when a BRAC commission voted to permanently shut it down. The official closing ceremony was held in 1999. During World War II, it was one of the largest Army installations, training approximately a half-million troops. After the war the Military Police Corps, the Chemical Corps, and the Women's Army Corps all operated out of Fort McClellan. Before its closure in 1999, it was a training ground for chemical warfare.

According to David Carpenter, director of the Institute for Health and the Environment at the State University of New York, the combination of toxic chemicals from Fort McClellan, the nearby Anniston Army Depot, and the Monsanto plant makes it the most contaminated place in the United States.

Decades of polychlorinated biphenyl (PCB) pollution had permeated the tree bark, and drinking water was tainted by heavy metals, solvents, and other hazardous waste from the trifecta of McClellan, Monsanto, and Anniston Army Depot. Stockpiles of aging and leaking Cold War-era chemical weapons are gone as of today, but arguably the damage had been done.

Fort McClellan in Anniston.

View from porch area at Ft. McClellan.

Vintage chair sits in a spotlight of sun that pours through the nearby window.

Signs for a disaster relief project kept in the basement.

Bed and wall locker in living quarters.

View from the top floor of one of the many vacant buildings.

Left: Member list of the 14th Army Band.

Below: Choose your own adventure: the fallout shelter or the exit.

Right: Fallout shelter.

Below: Fundraising goals seem to be met, but Ft. McClellan was shut down nonetheless.

Above: Curtains still on the windows inside.

Left: The clock forever at 5:43.

Above: Some things raise more questions than answers.

Right: American flag outside.

6

FUNLAND WATERPARK

No longer welcoming to visitors, Funland's broken slides, toppled light poles, desolate go-kart tracks bring visions of bad horror movies. While inside, your mind easily manipulates an innocent breeze into meandering footsteps stalking visitors through the fallen park. Presently, the only way out is over the fence topped with barbed wire.

In 2009, Funland's owner envisioned big ideas for the park that never came to fruition. In an article from The Times Daily, the new owners, SnowMasters out of Kentucky, reference a "water slide with snow falling around you, lasers and explosions interrupting your focus on a miniature golf course," and a human slingshot where "you put a person in a ball and shoot them. They come unattached and land in a big glove." It was set to reopen the same year in June, but never did.

Rumors from the locals vary as to why the plans for Funland failed. According to a few, the park functioning under the original owners was never fully up to safety standards and every year visitors would leave injured. Ultimately the financial burden of necessary renovations proved too steep.

SnowMasters never opened their vision for Funland. It shut its doors for the last time in 2011.

Another view from the skies. Junk boats line one side of the park.

Stairs leading up to the biggest slide at Funland.

Toppled light pole.

Go-kart track now full of leaves.

Broken slide full of water and leaves.

Desolate picnic area next to the water slides.

7

ALABAMA TRAINING SCHOOL FOR GIRLS

Park the car. Ditch the car. Walk a couple miles through the woods. A paved road in the distance hints at civilization, though a distant one, long forgotten. The pavement is a relief to tired, searching feet. The road turns and there you can see it, like a shining city on the hill, only more crumbling than shining, and more of a prison than a city. There's something inherently eerie about structures built in the 1930s—lead paint, asbestos, and mold, inadvertently malicious by design.

However, these things weren't the immediate threat to the twelve to eighteen-year-old girls housed there. A sign on the wall reads "safe area," but the Alabama Training School for Girls in Chalkville was anything but. A lawsuit brought in 2002 described disturbing patterns of sexual abuse and neglect. Girls incarcerated here were sent by family court judges for things like truancy, shoplifting, and drug possession. The lawsuit alleged that between January 1993 and June 2001, they were viciously mistreated. More than forty teenagers filed federal lawsuits against the State's Department of Youth Services, its administration, and several guards. According to a Marie Claire article, "the suits contend that, among other things, the girls were sexually assaulted, strip-searched by male guards, beaten, capriciously tossed into solitary confinement, denied medical attention, pressured to have abortions, and threatened with retaliation if they complained." A total of forty-nine plaintiffs would go on to win a massive $171 million lawsuit against the agency.

The reform school found its home in Chalkville, Alabama, in 1937. Built circa 1936, the school was part of a project created through Franklin D. Roosevelt's Works Progress Administration, a program designed to put people to work in an effort to end the Great Depression. The campus originally included cottages, an administration building, a hospital, dorms, and a chapel. Many of these stone structures are still standing, but in 2012, an EF3 tornado leveled quite a bit of the campus. Eighteen girls were residents at the time, and no one was injured. Today, the so-called dorms where the girls lived are still standing, and when you stand at the end of the long hallway light filters through each room's barred window and illuminates one after another. Standing inside one of the rooms, you can almost touch each wall from the center of the room. They were impossibly small cells with only a bed, a shelf, and heavy doors with several locks that latched shut from the outside.

Amid allegations of abuse and due to a lack of funding, the school shut down for good after it was hit by the tornado in 2012.

Alabama Training School for Girls.

Common area inside the school.

"Safe area" at the entrance of the cells.

Eerie living conditions inside a so-called dorm, which appears to be more of a cell.

Curtains still hanging from the windows.

Above: Entrance to the chapel on campus.

Left: Chapel window.

Trashed room inside the chapel.

Broken bathroom mirrors.

Above left: Sunlight filtering through room after room where the girls stayed.

Above right: Beautiful window of vines and peeling paint inside the school.

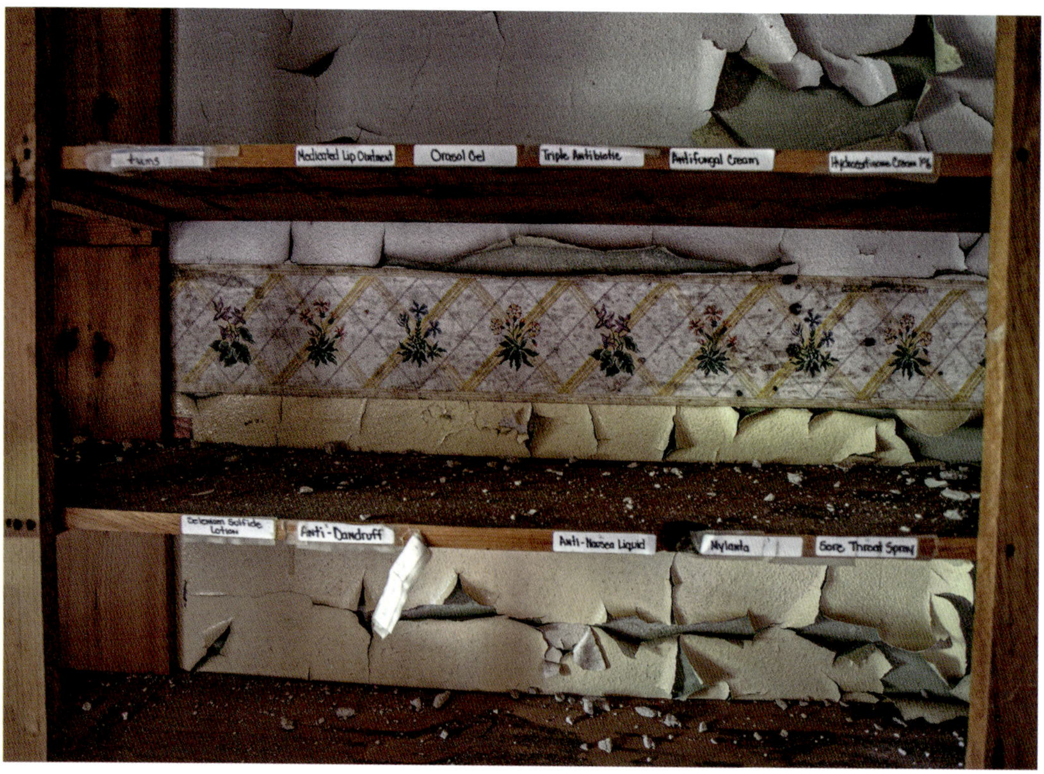

Covered in vines, but leading to a gorgeous view. It's easy to imagine people enjoying the view.

Above left: Vines creeping inside toward a hymnal left on the ground.

Above right: Strange pool or spring in a building on campus away from the rest of the buildings.

Door inexplicably thrown through a window.

Above: Vintage doorknobs at the Training School for Girls.

Left: Vines taking over a side building.

Vines and spiderwebs taking their space.

Busted light.

Outdated electric components line the wall.

More vines filling in the space where people no longer walk.

Another side building on campus.

In the basement of the school.

8

PINE TREE TRAIL RESORT

Completely ransacked and hardly more than a pile of rubble, Pine Tree Trail Resort is just barely standing. Vandals have laid waste to the resort, but it looks as if it were instead pummeled by a tornado. Inside the first building you come to, another piano lays on its side among the other debris.

Pine Tree Trail resort was originally developed as a timeshare resort in Bremen, Alabama. Facing legal issues, it was forced to shut down. It re-opened in the 1990s under a new name, Bremen Lakeview Resort. As of 2011, the resort was listed at nearly three million dollars. The property is sitting on seventy acres with beautiful views of Smith Lake. I often wonder exactly how many years it would take for it to completely collapse in on itself like a dying star. Climbing the soggy, rotting stairs leads you to the second floor. As with so many of these forgotten places, you can easily close your eyes and imagine it as it was when it was still functional. You can picture a couple leaning on the railing, taking in the view, having a drink to celebrate some turning point in their lives. Lean on the rail now and you would find yourself teetering on the edge of a long fall as the rotting wood surrenders to the weight. The wind blows and you feel the entire structure shift beneath your feet. Presently, it still stands, though the structural integrity is quickly losing its battle with neglect.

What's left of Pine Tree Trail Resort.

Another piano missing most of its ivory.

A room at the resort.

Vandals have trashed the resort on Smith Lake.

Covered in vines, but leading to a gorgeous view. It's easy to imagine people enjoying the view.

The view of Smith Lake from the second story.

Neglected pool at the resort.

9

WOLF SPRINGS ELEMENTARY SCHOOL

Visiting a school after hours is always strange. Absent of the raucous happenings of a school day, vacant schools are quiet and oddly still. Missing the footsteps of children clamoring about, other senses take the forefront. Without the familiar noise crowding out your other senses, you're instead able to smell the familiar mixture of scents of cleaning supplies, crayons, and pencil shavings. The quietness of an abandoned school is equally strange, but also feels slightly sinister. Instead of kids at home with an after-school snack, your mind imagines footsteps of ghosts, echoes of the past. Wolf Spring School was built in 1936, and today glass litters the old, formerly beautiful wood floors. The sunlight spills through the emptiness where windowpanes once were and shards of glass quiver with light.

The old rock school was built entirely with volunteer help with only the supervisor being a paid position. The land where it sits was donated in order to consolidate four other local schools into one. The grades taught there ranged from first to eighth. After the school closed, the building was used as a community center. Voting ballots from past elections are scattered throughout the rooms. As I made my way through the school, I collected and arranged the pieces of a smashed guitar from each room I visited. It seemed that once it was no longer of service to anyone, it served as a hangout for bored teenagers with nowhere else to go.

Wolf Springs Elementary School.

Entrance to the school.

Chair in the hallway. Beautiful wood floors.

Gym area inside with its ceiling starting to collapse.

Above: Pieces of a guitar found inside.

Right: Vandalized classroom.

10

DESERTED TRAIN

Follow the overgrown tracks and about halfway down them. you'll come to an unused train. Desolate and unmoved for quite some time, it sits along the railroad, heavily vandalized and perhaps housing those with nowhere else to go. Its only value now is that it provides a decent shelter from the elements. Trees and brush lining the outside of the train make it difficult to discern where noises are coming from. With each new car you visit, you brace yourself for contact with someone taking shelter inside. The train seems to go on and on, and the diminishing daylight forced me to turn back. Wandering the rest of the way in the dark, I might not have made it out. It was one of the places I intended to revisit, but it has since been demolished. The only evidence of its existence is held in this book, among other places on the internet.

View from the outside of the caboose.

Overgrown railroad tracks.

Above: View from outside looking into the defunct train.

Right: Inside, the train is collapsing in on itself.

Vandalism covers every inch of the inside.

Inside the train.

11

WHITE HOUSE ANTIQUES

White House Antiques was one of those booth rental type businesses. It was the building you might need, but couldn't afford to both lease and keep the lights on. So instead, people paid rent to the building owner in order to set up a booth of their own things to sell. This arrangement typically works out well for everyone until you're met with chains on the doors, your things still inside. White House locked its doors suddenly with no notice to renters or patrons. Speaking with former renters, they'll tell you that they've not been able to contact the owner, or anyone associated with her. Ransacked by vandals, perhaps former renters, too, the antiques are gone and what remains are only broken pieces—an empty chest, shattered picture frames with soggy prints clinging to the backing, and unwanted books. An overturned piano (there's always a piano) missing its ivory lays beaten and broken as if it had been jumped for a debt it couldn't repay. Pianos are notoriously lousy renters. Weighing too much to be easily evicted, they squat where they are until time sees them out.

More than a decade ago, prior to being an antique mall, it was Barfield Nursing Home. If you were to step back in time to the first time it was left vacant, you would find the skeletons of hospital beds. Water dripped from the ceilings and bedding was left on the floors. The piano was still upright in the cafeteria and somewhat playable, though starting to show its age and neglect. Fingers toying with its keys echoed untuned notes down empty halls. Teenagers armed with flashlights would challenge one another to spend the night in the vacated rooms. Ultimately, Barfield relocated to a sound building nearby and continues to care for those in need of assisted living.

These two entirely different operations sat on a severely damaged foundation, forcing it to be abandoned again and again. All that persists are stories of ghosts.

Entrance to White House Antiques.

Fallen door at White House Antiques.

Nature blocking the exit.

An empty room inside.

Rose among glittering pieces of shattered glass.

Shattered and soggy framed print left behind.

Shattered and soggy framed print left behind.

12

BURTON MANUFACTURING/ FAIRWAY

Formerly the home of Burton Manufacturing, this factory in Jasper, Alabama, sits in the middle of a now residential area. The houses surrounding it are busy with young neighborhood kids running about mostly disinterested in the decaying building down the street. To them it has become part of the ordinary scenery, no different from the trees. A fence surrounds the empty building. Typically, the fences that enclose these places are unfinished, leaving a hole somewhere for those curious to see what's inside. Fences aren't cheap and I suppose the illusion of a place being properly fenced is enough to deter most from exploring any further than the street where it sits. However, spray paint on the walls inside is evidence of older kids venturing beyond their childhood driveways.

The sprawling factory floor is covered with intruding vines and debris from the upper floor where it's caving in. It's a massive building with an elevator shaft that's no longer of any use. The stairs are nearly as useless. Staying close to the wall where the stairs are slightly more solid, you can make it to the top. The second floor has walls of windows that entice you to come inside to see them all, but venturing too far past the landing is risky. The floor upstairs is mostly for looks at this point, as anything bearing too much weight will cause it to crumble. Back against the wall, you can shimmy along it a little way. Too far in and you feel the floor beneath your feet give, warning you to turn back.

Burton Manufacturing was founded in 1907. In its early days, Burton specialized in leather horse collars and harnesses, but later become well known for producing high quality golf bags. By the 1950s, Burton was producing approximately 15,000 bags per year. In the mid-80s, it had made bags for Ronald Reagan and Mikhail Gorbachev. And at one time, eighty-one percent of the bags used on the PGA tour were Burton bags. But in 2006, Forefront Holdings would acquire Burton. Forefront was part of the Stanford Financial Group, which was seized by authorities and charged with fraud in 2009. This effectively shut down Burton amid allegations that its parent company had been operating a massive Ponzi scheme. The Jasper plant ultimately closed in 1995, but vintage Burton bags can still be purchased online.

Burton Manufacturing in Jasper.

The factory overgrown and starting to collapse.

Light in an elevator shaft.

Switches inside the elevator.

Fans in the walls of a side room.

Window in a brick room inside the plant.

Trashed exit.

Chair left in the middle of the floor.

Second floor of Burton.

13

WHEELER GRAIN CO. GRANARY

The only obvious entry to this granary is welded shut, seemingly inaccessible to the adventuring types. There are two potential ins. One involves testing your luck and repelling in from the top—approximately 75 feet. The other is finding the not-so-apparent underground tunnel system. The latter is damp and cold, but a significantly safer option should you be savvy enough to find it. Once on the cusp, sunlight pours through the openings and leads the way to the strange echoes heard from inside what is left of the dome above. Rainy seasons prove difficult to navigate, as the mud is so thick along the way it seems determined to wrench the boots from your feet. Keeping close to the tunnel walls is your best bet. Running your hand along the cold cement, your heart stutters uneasily when you feel some of the protrusions twitch and shift away from your touch. Thousands of cave crickets have taken up residency in the absence of humans. A couple hundred feet in and another choice presents itself. Metal fencing of uncertain stability leans from the muddy ground to the floor of the dome above you. A cinder block sits intentionally positioned below a window-like hole leading to the same destination. Once inside the massive structure with its dome blown apart, every noise is amplified and echoed. Noises bounce off the walls and reverberate with odd distortion. The curved walls are steep and climbing them requires a running start. Coming back down is an uneasy dash to the bottom, hoping you don't lose your footing as gravity forces you to descend faster than you'd like.

Built in 1982, Wheeler Grain Company's granary, located next to the Elk River, west of Athens, was only operational for approximately three years. At capacity, it could hold a million bushels of grain. It was designed by Dr. Arnold Wilson, a civil engineering professor at Brigham Young University and a pioneer in the monolithic dome industry. Originally equipped with a dome, the granary is 150 feet in diameter, with a height of 75 feet. At present, the dome is gone, the door is welded shut, and it is only accessible by an underground tunnel system.

In 1988, the granary caught fire and the 300,000 bushels inside burned for months before ultimately causing the structure to explode. The explosion was said to have been heard from four miles away. Thanks to the structural integrity of the lower walls, the energy from the blast shot through the cement top. The pressure releasing in this way pulls debris back down inside the dome instead of throwing it outward. Exploding vertically as opposed to horizontally minimized the collateral damage to surrounding areas. No deaths were recorded.

The fire was said to be caused by methane produced by the grain not being properly eliminated. There have been many cases of silos and associated buildings exploding due to the air becoming laden with finely granulated particles, and just a spark can trigger an explosion powerful enough to blow a concrete silo and adjacent buildings apart. Sparks are typically caused by metal rubbing against metal ducts or static electricity.

The owners anticipated a potential explosion and were searching frantically for something to defuse the hazard. Attempting to inject a semi-truck load of carbon dioxide into the dome proved unsuccessful. It inevitably exploded some time during the night, leaving a hole at the top 100 feet in diameter. Locals who resided near the granary were uneasy about its closeness from the beginning. Some speculated that the fire might have been intentional, though there was no official evidence of that being the case. No longer in need of the storage space, the granary was never repaired but remains standing.

The Granary, sometimes lovingly referred to as the "Great Pumpkin."

Underground tunnel system is now the only way in.

Looking up from the floor of the tunnels.

A view from inside the underground tunnels.

Valve inside the tunnels.

Above: Inside the area where the grain was stored.

Right: The vertical explosion destroyed the dome of the granary.

14

SANTEK MACHINE SHOP

SanTek Machine Shop, located in Guntersville, opened in 1975 and has been closed for years. The sign on the door reads "gone to lunch." They've been at lunch since 2008. The building sits unused and unnoticed with odd things left. An old bingo machine sits out back and eye wash stations are bolted to the walls. Teddy bears and Christmas trees are among the things inexplicably left behind. It's not exactly used for storage, but the things that remain raise more questions than answers. The open factory space is mostly empty, with odd things lining the perimeter. Light spills through the ceiling and fools the senses on a sunny day when you might think someone still pays the power bill.

Gone to lunch sign still on the door.

Spiders making their homes on the flag.

A bingo machine found at the back of the SanTek building.

Eye wash stations are bolted to the walls.

Stuffed monkey creepily left behind.

Inside the SanTek building.

Christmas tree in an office area.

15

THE LOST STORIES

Sometimes there are no stories. Sometimes the physical pieces of things outlive the narrative. Sometimes stories die with the people who tell them. Houses are inexplicably left to rot in their owners' absence, children's toys become heavy with rainwater as kids move out and move on, and old rotary phones have their conversations silenced by new technology. I've included this chapter of miscellaneous things to showcase the places and things whose stories eluded me. You're likely to find plenty of physical evidence that a story existed at one time, but their histories are quickly lost to time and indifference. Details are lost should we fail to share them. With no record or rewind button, we must share what we want to see make it to subsequent years. As I write these final pages, already several of the places I've documented have been demolished. Intending to go back to revisit a few, I've learned that they're gone. Over just a period of months, the only evidence that remains of these places are the details in this book, the details in online blogs, and the photographs from those who lived or worked there. You can always revisit a physical place until that place is gone. Unable to revisit the time when it was still standing leaves you with an empty feeling in your stomach. The only way a story survives is if we repeatedly push it along through time by various modes of communication. Movement is the saving grace. We must never let things become too still, because nature will quietly devour what is stagnant enough to wrap its vines around.

Above left: Old gas pump with its insides exposed at a defunct service station.

Above right: House in the trees in Union Grove.

Porch view of the Union Grove house.

Beautiful ornate door to a house left unoccupied, shrouded by trees.

A doll and curtains still remain inside a forgotten house.

Handwritten love letters from the 60s found in an attic.

A strange log building in the woods. Its story evaded me.

Old soda bottles outside.

Shoemaker's tools.

Unwanted toys left behind.

A small church found collapsing on itself.

Another house left to rot in the woods.

Odd place seemingly used for storage now.

Haint blue ceilings of the church were said to ward off evil spirits.

The insides of the piano at Edna Hill Methodist Church.

Inside Edna Hill Church.

Ceilings collapsing in a side building on a farm.

The view looking out of a defunct farm building.

Nature taking back its space.

Above: Airplane mounted above an abandoned gas station.

Right: Closed in 2010, the twin-engine 1939 Beechcraft 18 is still there with only one prop that spins with the wind.

ABOUT THE AUTHOR

Mary Posey is an award-winning photographer out of Alabama. Her passion for photography dates back to time spent in a darkroom as a teenager. Presently, Mary resides in a small town on the outskirts of Huntsville. She's often spotted on the floor of a decaying building surrounded by shattered glass and the first rush of plant life creeping back in to reclaim the structure's space. Mary's goal is to combine her passions of photography and urban exploration in an artistic attempt to show others the often unseen and rarely understood side of places society seems to have forgotten. Mary's work can be found online at www.facebook.com/studio256al and @mary.posey on Instagram. Prints for purchase can be found at studio256.smugmug.com.